How to Grow Kiwi Vines

Step-by-Step Guide On Growing Hardy Kiwi Plants in Colder Climate

ANASTASIA FOX

TABLE OF CONTENT

INTRODUCTION

Hopefully, this books includes the information you are seeking on learning how to grow your own kiwi vines in colder climates. We will cover the different aspects that you need to be aware of in order to become successful in developing your own kiwi vines. Within these pages, you will discover information that will help to guide you on how to begin growing and maintaining your kiwi vines. It is an interesting read even if you are not planning to grow kiwi vines, but what to be more informed about kiwifruit and its history of how it came to be such a widely favorite fruit throughout the world's commercial markets.

May you enjoy expanding your gardening skills by adding kiwi vine growing to the list. I wish you many happy years of fun kiwi harvests, and hope the tips and advice to successfully grow kiwi vines will benefit you greatly! You can always look back into the book when you need it through the season, to remind you of the specific chores you need to complete to help ensure that your kiwi vines will be healthy and robust, baring plenty of fruit at harvest time for you and your loved ones to enjoy!

Chapter 1 – Where Does the Kiwi Fruit Come from?

Some of us know the kiwi fruit as the Chinese gooseberry, that is a sweet tasting fruit that grows on kiwi vines. The kiwi fruit actually originated from the northern and eastern forests of China, where it was not cultivated and was just thought of as a wild plant. However, in the 1900s the seeds of the kiwi were transported to Europe and the United States and were grown into vines. It was initially intended to be an ornamental plant, to decorate pergolas in gardens and not to be produced for its fruit.

The kiwi vine produces lovely edible fruits that are about the size of a walnut, that have a similar flavor to ripe gooseberries. It is a very handsome looking plant with its appearance adding great visual value to any garden. Kiwi seeds were also transported to New Zealand, where vines were first grown outside of the town of Wanganui, located on the west coast of the North Island. Before long the growers had grown vines that had successfully fruited and began to raise the seedling and choose the plants that proved to be the best producing types.

The most important variety of kiwi that is grown today for commercial reasons was developed by Hayward Wright in 1928, known as the Hayward Kiwi. By the time the year 1940 came around, there were many plantings of kiwi vines. The kiwi became commercially exported in 1953 to North America, Japan, and Europe. The word kiwi started in New Zealand. It had been changed from Chinese gooseberry in the year 1959 to improve recognition and sales abroad. The popularity of the kiwi grew quickly worldwide with its production reaching close to 3.000.00 tons of kiwifruit produced per year, compared to 40.000 tons in 1983 and 300 tons in 1937.

Growing kiwi in my area

When most of us visualize the growing of kiwifruit, we tend to picture a tropical location. We presume something that is so exotic and delicious must come from an exotic area, right? But if the truth be told you can grow kiwi vines in your own backyard, even if it is located in zone 4. There are hardy varieties of the kiwi that can be produced in colder climates. With the tips in this book, you will be able to grow your own hardy kiwi plants in no time!

Kiwi for cold climates

The larger, fuzzy, oval kiwi fruit that is commonly sold in grocery stores tends to be grown in zone 7 and higher. There are smaller hardy varieties that can be produced by the northern gardeners in zone 4. The smaller varieties of kiwi are often referred to as kiwi berries due to the smaller fruits that develop in clusters on the vine. The smaller varieties of hardy kiwi offer the same flavor as their larger, fuzzier, and less hardy cousin, Actinidia chinensis. It also tends to be packed with more vitamin C than most citrus fruits.

The Actinidia arguta and Actinidia kolomikta are hardy varieties of kiwi vines suitable for growing in zone 4. Be sure that you have both male and female kiwi vines. Only the female plant will bare fruit, but a male plant is needed nearby for pollination. One male plant for every 1-9 female kiwi plants is needed. The A. kolomitka female can only be fertilized by a male A. kolomitka. The same goes for the A. arguta female can only be fertilized by the male A. arguta. The only exception to this is the variety 'Issai,' which is a self-fertile hardy kiwi plant variety. Below is a list of other hardy kiwi vine varieties that need a male for pollination:

- 'MSU'

- 'Arctic Beauty'

- 'Meades'

- 'Geneva'

- 'Ananasnaja'

In this book, I am presenting the hardy kiwi, but keep in mind that each species has many varieties, so I suggest that you check in nurseries for individual requirements. You can also use plant hardiness maps as a guide to see if you can grow kiwi vines based on the zone that you are located in. Check online for plant hardiness zone maps for your area or country.

Kiwi Berries

Hardy kiwi

The kiwi cultivar that is known as A. Arguta, or Hardy kiwi, is generally hardy to about -25°F (-30°C), USDA Hardiness Zones 4 through 7, and need about 150 frost-free days for the fruit to ripen. The size the fruit is about the same size as a large grape and is not fuzzy. The fruit can be consumed with the skin on.

Arctic beauty

This cultivar A. kolomikta, is also known as Kolomikta, it can tolerate temperatures going as low as -40°F (-40°C) and it requires around 130 frost-free days to ripen. It also does best in areas that are partially shaded and can grow in the regions that are slightly more alkaline soil (pH 5.5-7.5) as compared to other kiwi varieties. It is hardy to USDA Hardiness Zone 3. It may have random patterns of pink and white on its leaves.

Fuzzy kiwifruit

The most common variety of kiwifruit that is found in grocery stores is the Actinidia deliciosa cultivar – Hayward. If you are located in an area that gets about 230 frost-free days per year, you can grow it. It needs about 30 days of cold weather approximately around 30°F (0°C) to produce flowers. It can tolerate temperatures down to 10°F (-12°C) when the plant is dormant. The Hayward kiwi is suited to be grown in USDA Hardiness Zones 7 through 9.

Chapter 2 – What You Need to Begin Growing Your Kiwi Vines

Necessary requirements for growing your kiwi vines

Below I have made a list of the requirements that will be necessary for you to grow your own kiwi vines in a colder climate. These things range from soil consistency to planting for you to become more familiar with the growing requirements that kiwi vines prefer.

Soil

The type of soil that you have in your area is certainly going to be an essential element when it comes to successfully growing your kiwi vines.

Soil that is deep well-draining soil and rich in organic matter is the type of soil that kiwi plants will thrive in. The soil should be acidic, with an optimal pH of approximately 5-6.5. Kiwi plants can tolerate neutral soil. If the soil has more alkaline (pH = higher than 7), the plants leaves will show nitrogen deficiency (by turning yellow), and the vines will not grow very well.

It is essential that the soil you are growing your kiwi vines it is well draining. If the roots of your kiwi vines become waterlogged, they can develop problems such as phytophthora crown rot. Yellowing of the leaves is a symptom that there is poor drainage or too much water. The growth of the plant can be inhibited, and it can be damaged if the roots are waterlogged for a couple of days. Hardy kiwis can tolerate wet soil better than other varieties.

If in your area you have a problem with wet soil, or water not draining or from a high water table, you can attempt to create mounds or a raised bed and plant your kiwi vines so that the roots will stay drier. Try to develop swales to lead the water away from the plant base.

Young kiwi plants are susceptible to imperfect soil and site conditions, because of this some growers grow their kiwi plants for 1-2 years in containers before planting them in the garden. It is essential that they are watered frequently and are produced in quality soil. One added benefit to growing your kiwi plants in containers is the ability to transfer the plants indoors for protection against extreme cold, as the danger of frost or low temperatures could damage your young kiwi plants.

Location selection and protection against sun, wind, and frost

Sun:

The cultivar Hayward requires a sunny position, but they are able to tolerate a little bit of shade. Hardy kiwis are more capable of enduring shaded areas better. The amount of sun that a plant gets is going to have an effect on the amount of fruit production and quality—best fruit production is reached in a location in full sun.

The trunk can be damaged by the sun during the winter because it is not shielded by leaves. To help protect the trees during the winter months you can wrap the trees in burlap or other material, or they can be planted in areas that will offer some protection against the winter sun, such as near trees or buildings. You can also paint the trunks with 1:1 mixture of white latex paint and water. Make sure that there is no toxicity in the paint.

Wind:

You want to make sure that the plants are going to be protected from strong winds, since winds are capable of causing damage to long shoots in spring and summer. You can tie the shoots next to support wires to help prevent wind damage from occurring.

Cold:

The vines can suffer from cold damage when the temperatures drop when the vines are not fully dormant (in autumn or late winter). This can cause damage to the trunk. This can kill young vines and can cause older plants to weaken. As the plant ages, it's sensitivity to cold decreases.

You can provide frost protection by wrapping the trees in burlap or other material. For the plant to harden off for the upcoming cold months, it needs to be exposed to some cold at the beginning of the winter season.

Prime sites are raised south or south-west facing slopes, but kiwi is also able to grow on sites that are more orientated towards north when there is a chance of frost in the area. With northern facing sites they can help to delay early growth in spring, which can be damaged by late frosts. To try to avoid frost injuries do not choose low areas and cool sites where cold air can stay to plant your plants.

When severe cold spells occur they can kill a grafted vine past the graft union, so self-rooted plants are recommended for frost sensitive areas. You can allow suckers from self-rooted vines that were cold-injured to be allowed to grow from below the part of the plant killed in winter. If you are in an area where the temperatures are too low to grow fuzzy kiwi variety like the famous Hayward, you can select the hardy kiwis or arctic beauty. All species of kiwis young shoots are sensitive to frost injuries, so some form of frost protection is still needed in frost-sensitive areas. You can use mulch to help prevent cold damage.

Kiwi plants have male and female plants

For you to get fruit from your kiwi vines, you are going to have to plant at least one male and female plant. Only the female kiwi vines bear fruit. Some cultivars can self pollinate and do not need a male pollinator, but the fruit tends to be bigger and yield more fruit when it has been pollinated by a male. When you have good pollination, this results in more seeds being produced, and with more seeds, you are going to have bigger fruit.

To help ensure good pollination you will have to plant male and female plants of the same kiwi species, and they need to be flowering at the same time. It is essential to have the same species because the different species of kiwis do not cross-pollinate and with the different varieties there are those that flower early and late. On average one male plant is needed to pollinate 6-10 female plants. If you have more male plants, this can increase productivity as more female flowers are going to be pollinated.

If you are short on space, you can choose to graft a male plant onto a female to give you a couple of male canes for pollination. One kiwi vine needs at least 25 square meters, for it to grow normally and produce fruit. A common mistake made by growers is to plant too many plants in a small area. This results in numerous and vigorous shoots as well as the unnecessary cost of buying more plants than needed.

Planting and spacing your vines

Plant your bare-rooted stock in early spring, make sure that the roots do not dry out while you are waiting to plant them. Vines that you are growing in a container can be planted throughout the year except during the high temperatures of midsummer as the hot elevated temperatures can be stressful to the vines. When you are planting your vines, you might want to add some slow acting materials like rock phosphate, compost, or kelp meal, but do add nitrogen-rich fertilizer as it will burn the roots of your vines.

Give your newly planted vines water after planting them. Plant the kiwi vines as deep as they were when they were in the pot. Space the plants about 15 ft (5m) apart when you are using a T-trellis system. Leave about 20 ft (6m) between the rows. The male plant does not have to be close to female vines. You can have them planted up to 50 ft (15m) apart.

You can plant your Hardy kiwi variety can be planted closer than the Hayward, as they are not very vigorous. Plant your Hardy kiwi vines about 10 ft (3m) apart. When you are planting your vines in a row choosing a south-north direction will give optimal sun distribution as every row will receive the same exposure to the sunlight.

Watering

Kiwi vines to do not like to stand in water, they still need to be watered regularly. The plants need to have adequate rainfall during the summer if not you should consider irrigation. If you mulch around the plants this will help to retain water.

During the summer is the most crucial time to water the plants as this is when they are most stressed. You can water your plants up to 2 to 3 times a week. You can water younger plants even more regularly. You may want to consider drip irrigation as it saves the most water, but make sure that you are not watering directly on the crown as this can cause it to be too wet and develop root rot.

During drought, kiwi plants can become very stressed causing the leaves to turn brown and fall off. It can also cause the number of blooms to be reduced, as well as reduce the size of the fruit and cause the fruit to fall off.

Mulching

Using mulch on your plants will help to keep them healthy as it retains moisture, and will help regulate soil temperature and control weeds. Add about 3-4 inches (8-10cm) of mulch around the base of your plants. You can use things such as wood chips, bark, and well-rooted compost.

Pollination

The kiwi flowers are pollinated with insects, such as bees. The kiwi plants do not produce nectar to attract pollinator insects. The plants only produce pollen. The female kiwi plants produce fake pollen, which can't be used to pollinate, to attract the bees. Pollination happens when an insect transfers male pollen to the female flower. The more pollen that the insects transfer results in more seeds being pollinated. This leads to bigger kiwis being grown.

Identifying your plants

If you are not sure what plants you are growing (male or female), then wait till the first kiwi flowers appear in the spring. The female kiwi flowers have a white pistil; the tall structure in the middle of the flower that receives pollen. The female kiwi flowers are generally larger. The male plants produce more flowers and do not have a central pistil as they only produce pollen.

Support for your kiwi vines

Your kiwi vines will thrive and will need strong support to climb into. They will not be able to grow without support. Many kiwi growers use a T-bar or a pergola system, these can be made to run up any structure at home.

You need to take care of your kiwi vines as they can grow quickly and overgrow their trellis is they are left unattended, if the shoots are not pruned regularly it can become a tangled mess. Pruning and regular maintenance of your vines can be rewarded with a big healthy harvest and vines that look healthy and strong.

Trellising

Kiwi plants are rampant plants and their trunks never come sturdy enough to hold the plants up off the ground on their own. You need to train your plants to some kind of support that is sturdy and allows the plants to have space to grow.

Commercial kiwi tree growers use trellis that is about 6-foot high post and a 5-6 foot wide cross piece. The supports for the plant are spaced about 15 to 20 feet apart. You can stretch wires horizontally about every 12-inches (30cm) between 6-foot-high T-bar supports. This will provide plenty of space for your kiwi to grow and thrive and also allows easy access for harvesting and pruning the vines. Space rows 15 ft apart.

A pergola system is a type of trellis where the vines are trained to a stable, overhead layer covering the entire vineyard. You can convert the T-bar system to pergola by stringing wire across the rows at every 30-inches (80cm). You can set rows up about 20 ft apart. You do not have to create elaborate trellises at home as the kiwi will grow up many different structures. The pergola structure offers a solid canopy, whereas the T-bar system has spaces between the rows of vines.

Chapter 3 – Multiplying Your Kiwi Plants

Planning how to multiply your kiwi plants

If you are considering propagating your own kiwi vines, this chapter will be sure to offer you some useful tips. It is relatively easy to establish kiwi vines, so you can quickly give them to friends and loved ones as gifts. Just remember that it will take a few years before they will be able to bear fruit.

Sexual reproduction (seeds):

The easiest way you can get some female kiwi seeds is to buy some kiwi fruit and save the seeds. You need to clean the seeds and plant them into some moist well-draining soil. Soon you will have many new plants, but this is the longest way to get your own kiwi vines, and the results will probably not be great. A kiwifruit can have more than 500 seeds.

Here is why:

When you begin your plants from seeds, you will get a mix of traits from a male and female plant (male pollinates the female). Often when mixing traits, there can be a problem with many fruit species due to their genres are very heterologous. Due to large gene variability, there is only a small chance that the offspring will inherit all of the correct gene combinations which make the parent line a great producer.

Propagating by seed is not the best method as the plants' traits are unknown until it flowers and produces fruits. This whole process can take up to an incredible 7 years! So, you should not expect to get the exact taste and look of the Hayward kiwi when you plant Hayward seeds.

For this reason propagation from seed is mostly used for producing rootstock for grafts to propagate proven varieties. It can also be used for producing new cultivars, with new genetic combinations. Growers that are growing large amounts of vines can afford to check thousands of plants to see if they will be good producers; usually, most of them are not. You can purchase an excellent known variety from a nursery.

Micropropagation

This involves growing many plants using modern plant tissue culture methods usually in a laboratory type of setting, but it is time and recourse consuming. Most regular growers do not have the resources or time to propagate like this. This process involves cutting the plant material in small parts and let it grow on a well-defined medium in a sterile environment. The individual pieces slowly begin to take root and start to develop into individual plants, which can then be transplanted into soil.

Cuttings

Doing cuttings is not considered the preferred option as they don't develop a strong root system and are also prone to attack by crown-gall, but they are easy to do.

You can use softwood and hardwood cuttings to propagate kiwi. You can make softwood cuttings from late April through July. Cut the shoot into segments just below each leaf node, then dip them into a root growth hormone and plant in a well draining soil. Water them regularly. The softwood cuttings should root in a couple of months.

For your hardwood cuttings, the plant needs to be dormant. That is from autumn to late winter, the period where the plant does not have leaves. I use the wood from pruning the vines, and I cut it into about 5-7 inch (15-20cm) long segments and stick them into the ground so that there is about 2/3 of the vine in the ground. Make sure to put the basal end into the ground and to mark what the variety of plant it is. You may also want to try using rooting hormone for a better outcome. There should be buds on the plants in spring, and they will eventually root. Be careful of the strong sun as it can quickly kill them as their roots are not developed. Remember to keep the soil moist.

You should write down what variety and sex of the vine you propagated so you will know what plants you will plant or give away.

Grafting

The preferred method for reproducing is grafting for kiwi vines. The best time to graft is in the spring. This process involves attaching a piece of 1 plant onto another and is left to grow. The base only makes roots, and everything above the ground comes from the attached plant. The base is what is called the rootstock and is usually from seedlings. The plants grow from one year in the nursery before they are ready to be grafted.

For plants that you are interested in cloning, collect scion wood from vigorous shoots produced in the previous season with well-developed buds. You can collect scion wood in the late winter and stored in the fridge in a plastic bag with some wet moss to keep the base moist.

When you are whip or wedge grafting, choose scion wood and rootstock that are roughly the same diameter. When whip grafting a diagonal cut is made across the wood that is in an N like fashion. The rootstock is cut in the same fashion, and the joints are connected. This type of grafting is the best as it allows the most cambium to be connected.

When wedge cutting the cut to the scion wood is done in a V like fashion and inserting the pointy end into a wedge made by splitting the shortened rootstock vertically. Then you insert the scion, so the cambium layers of rootstock and scion are touching (the area close to the bark). Even if the rootstock and scion wood are not the same diameter, you can graft them. Just connect the cambium layers on one side. With the T-budding only a bud is inserted into a T-shaped cut made into the rootstock.

You need to bind the grafted section with raffia or polyethylene tape and seal it with grafting wax, or you can just tie it with grafting rubber. You want to plant the grafted vines above the union of the graft so that only the rootstock will produce roots.

Vegetative propagation

With this particular method, plants are grown from parts of the parental plant. The parental plants usually have good traits and are great fruit producers and pollinators. By propagating them, you can get exactly the same traits in your new plants. When you clone the plant, you can make many new plants. So, when you are buying the cultivars of kiwi from a nursery, you will get cloned plants with known qualities.

Chapter 4. Maturation, Harvest and Storage of Your Kiwis

When growing kiwi vines one of the most critical steps is the storing of your harvest. You will find that you can quickly have more kiwis than you can eat in a month, so you need to store them well in order for them to last through the winter season. If you are not able to store them well, then give them away to family and friends.

Maturation, harvest, and storage of kiwis

When it comes to kiwi fruit, it is difficult to tell when it is ready to harvest. It is picked by hand. The commercial growers of kiwi measure the sugar in the fruit to determine when it is ready to pick. When growing your own kiwi at home, you can cut the fruit open and see if the seeds are black. If they are black, then the fruit is ready to harvest.

Usually around late September to the beginning of early frosts is when kiwi are ready to harvest. Kiwi fruit can mature on vines, but they can not be stored for long. Keep in mind that Hardy kiwis do not ripen uniformly so you will need to check your vines periodically to harvest the ripe fruit.

During harvesting, take the kiwi and hold the fruit and rotate it slightly to remove it from the stem. Store it carefully in a collection box because fruit that becomes damaged will not store so good.

Storing kiwi longer

To store your kiwis longer you need to harvest the fruit when they are still hard and store them at low temperatures. Kiwis can be stored between 3 to 5 months if they are stored in optimum storage conditions which would be at a temperature between 32° F to 32.9° F (-0.5° C and 0° C) with a relative humidity of 90 to 95%.

The lower you can get the storage temperature without freezing the fruit the longer they will keep. Do not store kiwi with fruits such as pears, apples, and bananas...as they produce ethylene gas which causes the ripening process to quicken.

If on the other hand, you want to eat them then place them at room temperature and next to fruit that produces ethylene gas and they will quickly soften and ripen.

Fruits that produce ethylene gas are:

Cantaloupe, mangoes, nectarines, green onions, blueberries, ripe bananas, apples, apricots, avocados, peaches, passion fruit, plums, prunes, tomatoes, and potatoes...

Chapter 5. Taking Care of Your Established Kiwi Vine

Fertilizing

Kiwis require a high nutrient content, particularly for potassium and nitrogen. You can use general purpose fertilizer (ratio 10-10-10), or you can look for other high nitrogen fertilizers with trace elements. It is recommended to use fertilizers that are formulated for citrus and avocado for fertilizing kiwi plants. The yield should be improved when you apply fertilizer as well as vine health.

In the first year, you should not add the fertilizer as younger plant's roots are sensitive and can easily get burnt. Root burns can also occur when concentrating fertilizer near the trunk. Leaf necrosis is a symptom of root burn.

During the spring season fertilize with nitrogen-rich fertilizer such as ammonium nitrate or urea, subsequent fertilization can be done in early summer. If nitrogen is added late in the season, it could cause the fruit to store poorly. Addition of organic matter helps to benefit the kiwi plants; this can also help to improve the soil. It is a good idea to add well-rotted manure or straw.

Apply the recommended amount of fertilizer around the root zone, not just the trunk. Then water so that the roots can uptake the nutrients.

Leaves—revealing problems

If you discover that your kiwi vine leaves are turning yellow, it might be an indication of a mineral deficiency. Yellow leaves are usually a sign of nitrogen deficiency, but can also be a sign of magnesium, potassium, or phosphorous deficiencies. To make a proper evaluation you will need to do a soil test.

On the other hand, brown leaves are caused by too dry soil/or sun damage to the leaves.

Pruning

To help guarantee that you will have a good harvest and healthy kiwi vines are pruning. Pruning helps the vines from becoming a tangled mess and also allows enough light to penetrate the canopy. When you have a good canopy structure, it helps you to grow bigger fruits. When you prune it also helps to encourage new vine growth which is important as new wood produces flowers in the following year.

The pruning process for male and female kiwi vines is different. With the male kiwi vines, they are only needed for their flowers that pollinate the female flowers. Once flowering is finished you can prune back the male vines to current year shoots that will produce flowers the next year. Male vines do not need to be pruned in winter, however, female vines also need winter pruning. The winter pruning is done to remove canes that fruited to allow new growth for the next year's harvest.

It is essential that you plan how you are going to grow your vines. Usually, an established kiwi vine consists of fruiting canes, cordon, and trunk, so it is essential that you have your pruning planned from the planting on. You need to tie the vines so they are supported, and must be pruned once during the growing season and once in the dormant season. If you leave it too late in the winter season to prune it can lead to sap bleeding from cut areas, but it usually is not harmful.

Training your kiwi vines

You should prune your kiwi vines right after you have planted them. Plant your vines right after the danger of frost has passed. Cut your kiwi vine back to about 6-12-inch (15-30cm) long, vigorous shoot. Choose one strong, vigorous shoot to be the main leader and allow it to grow. Tie it next to support it.

To make sure that the new vines do not sag and brake you need to make sure that the support is as tall as the trellis. You want to make sure that the vine does not grow around the support, but next to it. To prevent wind damage to new young shoot tie it regularly. When the vine reaches the middle trellis wire cut off the growing tip. Cut just below the wires so that growth of lateral shoots will be promoted, which will become cordons.

The two lateral shoots should be trained in the opposite direction along the middle of the trellis wire, by tying them along the wire. Make sure to cut all new shoots that develop from the trunk. Allow the cordons to grow to about 7 feet (2.1m) or when they have filled their allotted space, then cut off the tip. Cordons will be the main frame from which your new fruiting canes will develop.

The fruiting canes will grow across the wires. Make sure to space the canes every 8-12-inches (20-30cm) on opposite sides of the cordon, and try to choose the healthiest canes. If you have more canes, prune them back during the winter pruning. To try to prevent wind damage tie each fruiting cane to the side wires.

First year of growing your kiwi vines

During the first year of growing your kiwi vines cut off any side shoots and allow only a main vine to grow. Secure it by tying it to support to prevent any damages to your vine. Once it reaches a couple of inches below the trellis wire, cut off the tip to help promote the development of the lateral growth of your kiwi vine.

Second year

During the second year of growing your kiwi vines leave only two cordons to grow along the wire and cut off any new shoots that appear from the trunk.

Third year

During the third year of growth, there should be new growth appearing from the cordons. Make sure to prune the longer vines to about 20-inches (50cm) and remove the vines that are too close together as this will cause the plant to be too crowded. Leave about 8-12 inches (20-30cm) of space between the canes.

Fourth year

By the fourth year of growing your kiwi vines, the framework of your vines has been established. Now you need to prune out and shorten the vines yearly so that you can keep the framework you made. If you want to straighten your vines you can tie them down to the wire; this will also help to prevent wind damage to your kiwi vines. Now your vines are ready for next year's harvest.

Winter pruning your kiwi vines

During the winter season, the best time to prune your kiwi vines is when the temperatures are above 32° F (0° C) and before the kiwi buds begin to swell. This is usually in January or February but can differ, depending upon the weather conditions in your area. Only the female vines need to be pruned in the winter whereas the male vines only need to be pruned during the summer.

Cut the cordons back to their allotted length during the winter prune, and cut back the cane that fruited to a few buds beyond the spot where they fruited. The next season the young canes will bear fruit. One fruiting cane is usually retained. The healthy shoots are pruned back to 3-5 feet (1-1.5m).

You also need to remove the old lateral canes that have been producing fruit for two to three years and also shoots that are causing damages, are twisted or weak.

Summer pruning

The main job during the growing season is to keep your kiwi vines in check. This is very important because the kiwi vines can grow up to 20 feet (6m) in a year. By pruning regularly, you will help to thin out the overgrown plants, and this will allow more sunlight to penetrate onto the fruiting wood. Make sure not to prune too much as exposed trunk and fruit can be damaged by sunlight.

Shoots that are growing beyond your trellis should be pruned. Remove any new shoots growing from the trunk, as well as remove any tangled vines, and also cut back excessively rampant shoots that will shade your plant. Once your kiwi fruits begin to form on the female vines, you can cut back the shoots to 4 or 5 leaves beyond the maturing fruit.

For your male vines prune off the lateral shoots and leave only new shoots. Remove approximately 70% of the previous year's growth. On the cordons leave short new lateral shoots with about 8-12 inches (20-30cm) between them. When you pruned during the summer, it helps to allow the vines to have maximum growth for next year's flowers.

Conclusion

I hope that you enjoyed this book and had found the information that I have provided in growing your own kiwi vines in a cold climate useful. I tried to include all the information I thought would be essential for you to use to become a successful grower of kiwi vines. I hope that you will have many years of healthy kiwi harvests that you and loved ones will be able to enjoy the fruits of your labor!

Made in the USA
Columbia, SC
06 July 2023

20109421R00026